The Gluten-Free Survival Guide

Essential Lifestyle Tips and Recipes to Help You Find Joy Again

Beth Oldfield

Beth Oldfield

www.glutenfreetutorbetholdfield@gmail.com

www.glutenfreetutor.ca

www.glutenfreetutor.com

www.betholdfield.ca

The Gluten-Free Survival Guide-Essential Lifestyle Tips and Recipes to Help You Find Joy Again —1st ed.

Published by Prominence Publishing

ISBN 978-1-988925-49-3

Contents

For my family,
Peter, Josh, Sarah and Jesse.
Your support and encouragement
lights my way.
Thank you for believing in me and for
sharing my food with love.

Introduction

"The secret of getting ahead is getting started." - Mark Twain

I wrote this book for you because I know what it feels like to be told that you suddenly can't eat gluten. You're overwhelmed because you find yourself in a sea of information when all you really want is a quick solution to help you get back to normal. You're looking for a new normal where eating won't make you sick. You're motivated to tackle this issue head-on so you can get back to focusing on your family and your work but you're not sure where to start. You're hungry for bread and pasta and pizza and brownies but you can't have them, and this makes you sad and mad at the same time!

I wrote this book for you because I've been in your shoes. Five years ago, my world was turned upside down too! I was a busy working Mom with three teenagers. I barely had time to eat, much less question everything that was going into my mouth and I would've given anything to have a book like this to lead me through the challenges easily. Sure, I had people hand me long, informative books on the subject but I needed quick guidance that would set me back on track.

The Gluten-Free Survival Guide will save you time, money and energy because you won't make the same mistakes that I made.

Each chapter explains one of my top ten tips in detail, why it matters and how you can proceed with ease. And because I know that you just want to be able to make a gluten-free, delicious dinner and dessert for your loved ones, I have included twenty of my family's favorite recipes.

I hope that this book makes your life a bit easier and that it continues to be a good resource for years to come.

My Story

*"I think you have DH- dermatitis herpetiformis, the
rash that celiacs get when they are exposed to gluten."
(MD Laura) - October 10, 2014.*

As hard as it was to accept, these words changed my life for the better because they put an end to a two-year long battle I had been waging against red, itchy spots mirrored across my body on my knees, elbows, buttocks, ankles, fingers, hips and upper back. It looked as though I had been bitten by a million mosquitoes. People were asking me where I'd been camping so they could make a mental note to avoid the area. The problem was the spots didn't disappear like bug bites but would turn into wounds that when scratched, would take two to three weeks to heal.

The doctors I'd seen over a two-year period couldn't figure out the cause. At first, I was told that I was allergic to my black spandex clothing, which as a fitness instructor was very upsetting, and then I was told that I had eczema. In each case, the diagnosis left me frustrated and no farther ahead.

When I spoke to Laura, a recently certified dermatologist about to open her own practice, I was relieved to hear that there could be an actual solution to my skin woes. After all, how hard could it be to avoid gluten? At the time, I had just turned forty-five. I was in great shape physically and used to handling unforeseen circumstances in both my work and personal life. I was no stranger to discomfort, and I was used to making sacrifices to achieve a goal! The truth is I had no idea how difficult my life was going to become, and I would've given anything to have a book like this to lead me through the challenges easily.

Now, five years into my gluten-free journey, I'm thriving, and I want to help people just like you find your joy again in cooking and eating and living. My mission is to help you avoid the pitfalls and problems that commonly arise as you shift into a gluten-free lifestyle.

As a fitness professional with twenty years of experience helping people reach their goals, I know how to break down challenges into bite-size pieces, so that 'getting there is half the fun.

Let's begin.

Chapter 1: Talk About It and Find Your Gluten-Free Tribe.

"Sometimes the questions are complicated, and the answers are simple." - Dr. Seuss.

What's the issue?
Your feelings are normal.

I know that you feel a sense of loss and deprivation on this gluten-free diet. It's one thing to choose to live gluten free but quite another to be forced into it because of an allergy. I know that you're afraid to eat because the symptoms of exposure to wheat are so adverse. I know that you're stressed because you must analyze everything you eat when you're not used to putting so much time and energy into yourself. The last thing that you want is to be a burden to anyone trying to cook for you and you're probably hesitant to ask others to eat at gluten-friendly restaurants because the food is usually more expensive.

In the beginning, I dealt with my feelings of loss and fear and stress by keeping to myself. I didn't want to ask my friends to change their favorite hangouts to suit me, and I didn't want to have to give the server the third degree in front of everyone, in order to learn what I could and couldn't eat. It seemed easier to just stop going out altogether. I felt lonely and scared to eat and I was trying to carry on as if everything was normal, all while trying to hide my intensely itchy skin condition. I sweat for a living, so this was by far the hardest part.

The truth is life is much easier once you start talking about your condition. What you focus on expands and this can be good or bad. I was ruminating on everything that I had lost instead of looking ahead to how much better my life could be. I was needlessly suffering in mind, body and spirit, which made my situation far worse.

Why does it matter?
Swapping One Problem for Another

You need to speak to your doctor before you make drastic changes to your diet so that you don't sacrifice your health and cause other problems. Before we discovered that I had DH, I had drastically reduced the amount of calcium in my diet by eliminating cow's milk because it made me feel terrible to drink it. I had not thought to talk to the doctor about this but the tests that I was put through to determine if I had celiac disease revealed that I also had Osteopenia. It is common for celiacs to also experience bone density issues because as my doctor explained to me, a gluten-allergy can result in malabsorption of minerals. Had I not gone to see my doctor; I may have ended up with Osteoporosis. Do yourself a favor and see your medical professional first before changing your diet because you don't want to swap one problem for another.

Keep to Yourself at Your Own Risk

After a year of feeling isolated and lonely, I finally answered the "how are you" question honestly and it changed my life. It was my sister's surprise birthday party and her adult kids were interested in what I was up to, so I told them about my itchy rash struggle.

"You need to talk to Mom. She has had that going on for years."

Turns out that my sister and I suffer from the same allergy, but she had no idea that the symptoms she was experiencing were linked to gluten. Our parents taught us to never complain about any of our health problems, and because there are seventeen years between Jane and I, she would not have thought to talk to her little sister about her situation. Jane tells her story below:

"I had been diagnosed by a dermatologist in the eighties and told that I suffered from a nervous condition. It sort of made sense because I was not a child who could sit still, and so this diagnosis seemed to fit. As a child my parents also felt I had a food allergy to tomatoes. When I entered perimenopause and menopause, the attacks became more frequent and the sores took longer to heal. My scalp was also a huge source of itchiness and I experienced major bloating. When my sister and I finally had a chance to talk and compare notes it became evident that being allergic to gluten would explain a lot of symptoms that I was experiencing. Beth started coaching me on what worked for her and I began cutting back on gluten. It was not long before I realized I felt much better without gluten in my life!" Jane Oldfield-Cosh

Speaking openly with Jane and her family motivated me to discuss my rash with others which helped me to discover that many of my friends and co-workers are also on a gluten-free diet. People started passing me magazines and cookbooks and before I knew it, I was surrounded by like-minded people. I can still feel the joy of that first event that I attended where all the food was gluten-free. I didn't need to ask any questions. I could completely relax and enjoy the company.

Talking openly about your allergy just means that you're taking charge of your health. You deserve to eat well and enjoy food just like everyone else and once I started sharing with others, I found my tribe. People love you and would rather accommodate you, than never see you again. Remember that.

Don't Become the Disease.

Yes, you must eat gluten-free but if you're celiac or you have DH, that is just something you must deal with, it's not who you are. I can remember feeling as though I had lost myself even though the only thing that had changed was my diet. I want you to take a few minutes to tell me about yourself so grab a piece of paper and a pen.

Who are you and what makes you unique? What activities fill your day and how are you making a difference in this world? Set a timer and write for five minutes non-stop.

Keep this paper either in your new cookbook or in your journal to remind yourself that you are still you, only better because you are now eating foods that support your health.

What you can do today
Four Quick Remedies

Your mental health is just as important as your physical condition. In time, your symptoms will disappear but there are steps that you can take today to feel better.

1. Exercise.

Exercise will make you feel good especially if you set easily attainable goals for yourself. Something as simple as a daily walk around the block done at a quicker pace than the day before, will make you feel as though you can conquer any of life's challenges. Get moving any way that you can but try to find an activity that you love because this will boost your mood. Take a dance, fitness and/or yoga class to help relieve stress and improve your mood.

2. Eat well.

My doctor has told me to avoid high glycemic foods because the spikes in blood sugar make us crave more sugar which leads to crashes in energy throughout the day. All of which is very stressful on the body and the mind. You really are what you eat, so do your best to put only clean fuel that is low in salt, sugar and fat into your body.

3. Visit your local health food stores.

Once you find one that you like, the owner can be an invaluable source of information and support. Many of them offer courses in nutrition and have an in-house dietician on hand to help you navigate your way through the products in their store.

4. Internet Support Groups/Magazine

Gluten Intolerance Group (www.gluten.net)
Celiac Disease Foundation (www.celiac.org.)
Gluten-Free Living (www.glutenfreeliving.com)
Living Without (www.livingwithout.com)

Chapter 2: Kitchen Set Up

"The flower that blooms in adversity is the rarest and most beautiful of all." - Walt Disney Company, Mulan

What's the issue?
Cross-contamination is a real thing.

When you suffer from a gluten allergy, you must remove all traces of gluten from your cooking environment. That doesn't mean that you have to move out of the house or kick your family to the curb, it just means that you have to set up your space so that it's safe for you when you're preparing meals for the family and yourself.

As I live in the country, ants and occasionally mice used to be my biggest concern in the kitchen but now it's wheat crumbs, especially because I share my kitchen with 'regular eaters' as I call them. It seems silly to think that you could have a reaction from just the crumbs left behind by a non-vigilant sandwich maker but trust me you need to become the crumb police.

In speaking with the owner of Louise Gluten Free in Dorval, Quebec years ago, Louise told me that the amount of gluten that can send her to bed for days with intolerable symptoms is the equivalent of one crumb in a bathtub of water. I bought a brand-new toaster for myself on the way home that very afternoon and I got strict about my kitchen set-up. Thankfully my symptoms are not that severe but, in my opinion, it is best to do everything you can to keep your food wheat free. Remember that your goal is to get rid of your symptoms so setting up your environment for success is key.

Why does it matter?
The Effects of Stress

We all know how it feels to catch a cold and recover, only to catch another cold shortly thereafter. I'm thinking of winter when viruses are everywhere. It's exhausting physically. I feel the same way about exposure to gluten which brings on an allergic reaction. On a physiological level, your body doesn't want to be waging a non-stop war on foreign invaders. It wants to live a relaxed existence. These recurrences can lead to stress, which leads to more sickness, which can lead to isolation and sadness, which can lead to making poor food choices. The trick is to not get on the merry-go-round in the first place.

What you can do today
Four Easy Steps

The steps are quite simple when it comes to removing gluten from your home environment.

Get Rid of the Gluten

1. Take everything out of the cupboard and put it all on the kitchen table. It seems a bit crazy but don't skip this step
2. Read each label looking for traces of gluten and make piles with gluten and without.
3. Give away the food that you no longer want to keep in the house. For me, this meant wheat flours and all baking supplies because I'm the only baker in the family. If you live with wheat bakers, just keep their stuff far away from yours and establish strict clean up rules.

Establish Your Gluten-Free Zones

1. Make the top shelf gluten free. Why? Because your stuff will be free from any crumbs that might fall from the top shelf. I ended up having two complete shelves and half of another. I took masking tape and wrote "Moms" on the edge of each shelf.

2. Use small cardboard boxes or containers that are small enough to fit side by side on the shelf and use them to hold gluten-free sauces, baking powders, baking sodas and vanilla. Each labelled "Gluten-Free."

3. All items that you use from the fridge need to have your name on them. You will need your own butter, margarine, mayonnaise, peanut butter, jams etc. Basically, anything that we normally stick a knife or spoon into could get contaminated by someone who double dips or scrapes the excess back into the jar. Honestly, double dippers are my biggest fear at parties etc. I recommend that you serve a big pile of dip onto your plate before anyone else gets at it and never go back.

Cook Safely

1. Dedicate, if possible, a section of counter that is for you and you only. I chose the area where the family preps their morning coffee which is only used by others first thing in the morning and never sees any food. Everyone knows that they are not to make their wheat bread sandwiches on that counter. So that area never sees a wheat crumb, ever. I keep my toaster in the corner of this area.

2. Buy your own kitchen tools and choose red if you can. I did this and it stops my family in their tracks long enough for them to remember, 'oh yeah that's Mom's strainer.'

3. You will need a strainer for pasta, cooking spoons and spatulas and flippers. You should have your own fry pan and pots as well, simply because people don't necessarily wash as well as you will, and traces of wheat can get mixed in with your food.

4. Get your own cutting boards and not just one because you will want helpers when it comes to chopping vegetables for dinner and you don't want them chopping on wheat boards. And store those boards on your counter or in your zone in the cupboard.

5. When at the stove, you need to use your tools for your food but keep them separate from the wheat food being prepared. So, this will mean separate forks for testing and spoons for stirring. To avoid any cross-contamination, try to cook your food on one side of the stove, with your utensils resting on that side. Again, it helps if your tools are a different color!

Bonus Tip

When doing your dishes, wash your equipment first and change the cloth before washing the rest of the dishes. Crumbs in the sink water can get stuck in the cloth and then you are essentially rubbing the wheat pasta residue all over your gluten-free tools. Buy some red cloths or some that are distinguishable as yours only so that the regular eaters won't wipe down their counters with your cloths.

If you have someone baking with wheat flour in your kitchen, I suggest that you not be there at the time and advise them to thoroughly wash the space afterwards. Flour rises into the air when it is mixed, and it lands on everything. Wheat bakers can drape towels around the mixer to limit the spread of flour.

Once you get set up and educate the family on the zones in the kitchen that are gluten-free, you will be able to relax.

Chapter 3: Baking Dos and Don'ts

What's the issue?
Food Waste

Cooking with flours other than wheat presents many challenges. There isn't one flour out there that can replace wheat on a cup for cup basis, for every single recipe you own. Instead you must keep several different flours on hand along with starches and gums to help replicate the texture of baking made with wheat. I didn't know this initially, so I ended up with scones that poured out of the bowl onto the pastry mat and then got tough because I added extra flour to thicken the batter. Cookies that crumbled and tasted so strange that I had to pitch them in the garbage instantly. Loaves that were heavy and uncooked in the middle, never having risen even a tiny bit. Pie crust that would not lift off the rolling pin in one piece.

I cried many tears in the beginning, but I never gave up and now I want to share some very simple tips and products that will get you baking perfectly right from day one.

Why does it matter?
Gluten-Free Expense

Gluten free products are very expensive, so you want to do your best to create edible food. For example, my favorite flour that I use for my muffins, pancakes, waffles and cakes is almost $20 CAD for a five-pound bag, so wasting it is quite costly.

You want to be careful how much you make and how you store it because gluten-free products do not stay fresh for very long. You can have some success in freezing portions, but my best baking is done to measure and eaten quickly. Plan accordingly, and you will not waste food and money.

You might decide to forgo baking altogether, but I encourage you to bake your own food (except for bread as I explain later) because processed cookies, cakes and muffins are often full of extra sugar and fat to improve the taste. The good thing about baking for yourself and your family is you can adapt the recipes to be a bit healthier than store bought treats. For example, I often replace granulated sugar with maple syrup, coconut sugar or honey.

What you can do today
Seven Successful Baking Tips

These tips should help you avoid many of the problems that I experienced initially when trying to bake gluten-free.

Start a New Cookbook

1. Get yourself a notebook and keep it handy in the kitchen because you will be searching for new recipes and after you try them, you will want to store them for later use.

2. Yes, you can do this electronically, but I encourage you to do it by hand because the recipe gets ingrained in your memory when you write it out onto paper.

3. I rate each recipe after I try it and make notes if I found that it turned out better than the last time, listing exactly what I did differently.

Don't Try to Wing It

1. I can't stress this enough. Follow the measurements exactly because non-wheat flours respond differently. If you're like me and like to cook with "a bit of this and a bit of that," save that for your savory dishes. Baking is a science and we can't stray off the path too much when it comes to gluten-free baking. Stick to the recipes until you are experienced. This is the best way to avoid wasting food, time and money.

2. Ingredients should be at room temperature before you start baking so this is not very conducive to 'winging it' behavior. You can warm up eggs in a hurry in a cup of hot water, while you collect all the ingredients. I warm milk in the microwave for a few seconds.

Start with These Flours / Starches / Gums and Powders:

Small bags are preferable when you are first getting started and remember to keep them in the fridge. I took over much of the door space of the fridge with my tiny bags of flour and I also kept some of the lesser used flours in a Ziploc bag in the freezer. Just remember to bring them to room temperature before using.

1. Almond Flour: I have found that this flour is amazing for making all sorts of lovely desserts. You can usually find it in bulk at Costco or other big box stores.
2. Arrowroot Flour
3. White Rice Flour
4. Brown Rice Flour
5. Sweet Rice Flour
6. Corn Flour
7. Tapioca Starch
8. Cornstarch certified gluten-free
9. Potato Starch
10. Xantham Gum or Guar Gum (Guar is made from beans so it might cause bloating just like beans do, so if you are susceptible maybe

use xantham gum)

11. Baking powder and baking soda certified gluten-free
12. Cocoa - certified gluten-free

A Word About Baking Pans

1. Dark pans cook the outside of the food faster and can leave the center underdone. You will have to adjust the temperature of the oven to account for this if you have dark pans or treat yourself to new ones and a muffin tin too.
2. Loaves need to be baked in smaller pans. I have had great success using 5.75 x 3-inch pans. Gluten-free baking doesn't rise as easily so the smaller pan ensures that it rises and that the middle gets cooked. My banana bread recipe fits into three of these smaller pans.
3. Cookie sheets should be lighter in color as well. I always line my sheets with parchment paper because some gluten-free cookies need to be completely cool before you can remove them from the tray, and this allows me to slip them off onto a rack and keep baking.

Let's Talk About Bread

I know you miss the texture and taste of fluffy white or brown bread. I know that a store-bought gluten-free loaf can cost upwards of $7 so I understand the motivation to want to save money, but trust me when it comes to bread, just buy it. You will save yourself tons of energy and money and it will never, ever taste like wheat bread. This is the one place where I insist on purchasing prepared loaves, at least until you feel confident about the rest of your baking prowess. I wasted so much money baking bread that was hard as a rock and tough to chew. You would think that baking bread would be easy but, in my opinion, it is the hardest item to perfect gluten-free.

The brand of bread that I absolutely love that delivers great texture and taste is Little Northern Bakery. It is made in British Columbia, Canada but you can find it in the gluten-free freezer section of most health food stores or order it online.

When I do splurge and buy a loaf of bread, I keep it in the fridge because it stays fresher longer. If you manage to find a good, freshly baked bread and cannot eat it all before it gets stale, I recommend, separating each piece with a piece of waxed paper and then putting the whole loaf in the freezer. Then you can easily remove one slice at a time.

Try to buy the wide sliced bread because it resembles regular bread and you won't feel like a kindergartener, eating a tiny sandwich.

A Word About Pie

I love pie. More than I probably should, and in the recipe section you will find my all-time favorite pie recipe but there are a few things you need to know before attempting to make it.

1. Chill the discs of dough every single time for at least an hour. No exceptions.
2. Roll the dough between two pieces of waxed paper. One on the bottom, and one on top.
3. If you are not able to place the crust easily into the pie plate because it is sticking to the waxed paper, you can try chilling it longer or just push it into place as if you were playing with Playdough. I have done this many times. It works quite well.
4. Keep one disc in the fridge while you battle with the other. They need to be cold to handle well.
5. Sadly, most gluten-free flour does not brown easily. Before putting the pie in the oven, brush with a bit of water. This should result in a crisp, brown crust. If the pie is browning too quickly, loosely cover with foil.
6. Remember that glute-free baking does not stay fresh for long so make sure to cover the pie with a food wrap.

Work with Room Temperature Ingredients

1. I said this before but it's worth repeating in case you jumped to this section. Warm up your eggs, milk, butter (unless cold butter is called for) and flour before you attempt any baking. The ingredients mix better.

2. You should however chill pie crust discs and cookie dough before baking. This will result in cookies that keep their shape and crusts that are easier to handle and are flakier as well.

Chapter 4: Hidden Gluten

What's the issue?
Manufacturers Don't Make It Easy

You would think that eating gluten-free would be as easy as just avoiding baked goods, but it's not. Some foods that you wouldn't think contain gluten, do because manufacturers use wheat as a filler. Don't assume something is gluten-free. You must read every label. It's time consuming but it can save you days or weeks of misery in the long run.

There are many different names for the gluten that causes my skin condition. In general, if you're following a strict gluten-free diet you must avoid wheat, barley and rye and possibly oats. Malt is often made from barley so you must avoid it, but malt can be made from other cereal grains, so you must verify the source. You would think that you would be able to eat cereals that are made primarily from corn or rice but unfortunately most of them are sweetened with barley malt and therefore off limits.

Why does it matter?
Cycle of Sickness

One of the most frustrating things for me when I first switched to eating gluten-free was buying products that I thought were safe when they were not. I would get a reaction but not understand from where. This can be hard on you emotionally as you are already limiting yourself and then it can be hard physically when an outbreak or symptom occurs. So, in the midst of feeling bad you must become a detective and analyze everything you ate the day before and try to figure out if the food was the culprit, or cross contamination.

In my case my skin eruptions can last for weeks, therefore I must be hyper vigilant during the healing process, so I don't inadvertently expose myself to more gluten and make the cycle last longer.

You also must be aware of conflicting information. For example, I found stated in one book published in 2014 by the Mayo clinic, that gluten-sensitive people should avoid medications with caramel coloring listed in the ingredients but then another book on the same subject, said that is a myth. So, the way I deal with this is to avoid the food and when I feel I can, I try it and see how my body reacts.

The name of the game is 'playing it safe', and at times it feels as though manufacturers aren't playing by the rules when they use fancy names for something that could make me sick. My biggest piece of advice is to read every label and be choosy about the foods that you are going to try.

What you can do today
Fifteen Essential Safety Tips

Here is a list of ingredients to avoid or scrutinize.

1. Wheat can appear on labels under unfamiliar names so when you're shopping carry this list with you. Hydrolyzed wheat protein; bulgur; dextrin; dinkle; durum; einkorn; emmer; farina; graham flour; kamut; semolina; spelt; wheat berry; wheat germ, wheat gluten, wheat bran, wheat starch; couscous; seitan;

matzoh; matzo

2. Wheat free, doesn't mean gluten-free.

3. Be wary of bulk bins because people can double dip the scoops and contaminate the food.

4. Avoid triticale which is a hybrid of wheat and rye.

5. Barley is used as a thickener in soups and stews. It's also used to enhance flavor so look for words like malt, malt vinegar, malt sugar or barley extract or flavoring and avoid these products.

6. Avoid commercial sauces and salad dressings or inspect for wheat additives.

7. Soups often have hydrolyzed wheat protein in them so read the labels carefully, or they have pieces of pasta in the broth.

8. Processed lunch meats can have wheat crumbs in them as filler.

9. Soy sauce contains wheat so you must use the gluten-free equivalent.

10. Scrutinize jam, jelly and marmalades.

11. Nuts, dried fruits and spices can be a problem because often they are sifted with flour to prevent sticking. I choose to use only certified gluten-free versions.

12. Chips and fried foods can be contaminated if they are fried in the same oil as items drenched in flour, or the ingredients added after cooking to spice them up may contain wheat.

13. Medications: Avoid packages with these terms: Wheat or wheat starch; caramel coloring; maltodextrin and modified starch, which could be cornstarch, but you need to check.

14. Communion wafers. The church may have a gluten-free version.

15. Beer is off limits unless it is certified gluten-free

16. Bouillon cubes need to be certified gluten-free

Chapter 5: Restaurant Dining

What's the issue?
Don't Put Your Health in Someone Else's Hands

I love to cook but not 365 days a year. Sometimes I want to sit in a fancy restaurant or just a regular restaurant and have someone serve me a delicious meal. This is what I miss the most about going gluten-free. Thankfully, I have found some local restaurants that cater to allergies but finding these places is hard work.

You can never assume that a server knows or cares about your allergy. On a few occasions I made it very clear to the server that I had an allergy and a wheat bun was still served to me on top of my food! One morning I decided to just order fruit salad and not bother telling the server about my allergy, and the fruit arrived topped with raspberry jam. This was not listed on the menu. I couldn't eat it because it could have been thickened with flour, but I also couldn't blame the server because I didn't ask enough questions.

Why does it matter?
Because You Matter

Sometimes we choose to eat whatever is served to us in a restaurant, even if we're unhappy because we can see that the server is overworked or very busy. Just keep in mind that if you don't speak up when mistakes are made with your food, you could end up sick for days or weeks.

My daughter has worked in the food service industry her whole life and she has always told me to speak to the server about my allergy every single time. The truth is they want us to have a good time and enjoy our food, so we give them a good tip at the end of the meal. Just be patient and kind when asking questions and you should be able to find something to eat in any restaurant.

On our anniversary a few years ago, I cried tears of joy because once I had informed the manager of Ottavio's, a popular restaurant chain in Quebec, Canada, about my allergy he did his best to make our night special. Ottavio's serves regular Italian food but they cater to people with gluten allergies. The owner served me their Italian Poutine. Unbeknownst to him, I hadn't had french fries in well over two years and to boot, it was served with lactose-free cheese! It was one of the best Poutine's I had ever had!

You go out to have a wonderful dining experience. You don't want to get sick, so take a few minutes to talk to your server or the manager before ordering. It makes all the difference.

What you can do today
Six Quality Questions to Ask Every Time

1. How do you steam your vegetables? (Sometimes this is done over wheat pasta while it is cooking)
2. Do you fry breaded products in the same oil as the french fries?
3. Do you have a separate toaster for gluten-free bread?
4. Is my food prepared on the same surface as wheat products? Grills, cutting boards etc. Think steaks, burgers, eggs and home fries.
5. What is served with the meal or the fruit?

6. What is in the salad dressing? If in doubt, just order some oil and vinegar on the side.

Chapter 6: Eating at The In-Laws

"Happiness is having a large, loving, caring, close-knit family in another city." - George Burns

What's the issue?
Standing Up for Your Health

I can remember how insulted my mother-in-law was when I turned down a large container of commercial, processed peanut butter that she wanted to give me to serve to our kids. At the time, I was just being health conscious. I had no food allergies and neither did the kids, but as a fitness trainer who tries to keep up on the latest health news, I had learned about the negative impact that trans fats were having on our bodies and how they actually result in unwanted weight gain and disease. When I tried to explain my reasons for not wanting the processed peanut butter, I learned something very important. Food is a very touchy subject between friends but most especially amongst family.

How can there be something wrong with bread? Bread has been a staple in the western diet since before I was born, and as a result it can be difficult to tell an older, uninformed member of your family that wheat products are virtually poison to you. The last thing you want to do is insult the people you love. In my case, my parents passed on before I developed DH but my father, who was the biggest POM bread consumer there ever was, would have laughed me out of the room and told me that I was being deceived if I told him I couldn't eat bread!

It's hard to turn down food that you know isn't safe for you. I have eaten many things that I was concerned would bring on my rash simply because I didn't want to cause a fuss or hurt anyone's feelings. I don't blame you for doing it but just know that it's far better to "go without, when in doubt."

I can remember feeling quite badly that I had to tell my brother-in-law that I couldn't eat his hamburgers, especially when they had waited for almost two hours for us to arrive at their BBQ. We had been delayed in traffic and my text, telling them that we were stopping for a quick bite and to go ahead and eat without us, had not gone through. We arrived at the party, fashionably late and already fed, to find members of our extended family famished and so happy that they could finally put the meat on the grill and serve us.

At first, I considered just forcing myself to eat no matter how uncomfortable I would be and then I inquired about what was in the burgers to be sure I could eat them safely. He listed the ingredients and I told him the bad news.

"I can't eat that brand of Worcestershire sauce. I'm sorry."

"There's no gluten in Worcestershire Sauce," he insisted.

"Yes, there is. So sorry. I can't eat the burgers."

I had to follow him into the kitchen where he pulled out the jar and then his expression fell.

"Oh crap. You're right. It has wheat in it."

Sometimes you must show your loved ones the ingredients list and go through a bit of a discussion, but it is worth it in the end.

Just to be clear, you cannot take the apples out of the apple pie made with wheat and eat them. This was the suggestion that a friend of mine made when I lamented at not being able to eat his dessert. It sounded like a great idea and I waffled for one moment, because his pie looked and smelled so good, but the wheat is baked right into the apples at that point. I've even turned down crackers when someone has gone to the trouble of buying them for me, if they put them in the same basket as the wheat crackers.

Before I got the courage to speak up for myself, I would've simply eaten the burgers because my Mom taught me to be polite, but now I know better. Still it is important to be kind when proving your case.

Why does it matter?
Practice and Patience Makes Us Healthier

The good news is that even though it is tough to advocate for yourself at the beginning, your family loves you and wants you to be healthy. If you're clear and educate your family about how they can feed you safely, the benefits are many. You will get practiced at speaking up and you will get smoother at asking for what you can eat, and you will be able to relax and enjoy the company of those who mean the most to you. I must admit that at first, I just avoided many gatherings because I couldn't bear having to disappoint people. It was easier to just stay home alone, but as we have discussed, this is the wrong path to take because it leads to isolation with a whole host of its own problems.

Getting sick is not in your plan, so don't sacrifice your health by eating food that you know is going to cause you an adverse reaction, simply because it was prepared by your best friend or mother-in-law. This will be an ongoing challenge.

What you can do today
Ten Recommendations

My sister-in-law, Karen, is the keenest learner when it comes to trying to cook for me. You will have lovely souls like these in your life and that is where you will learn just how much information you really need to give someone who is happy to prepare a meal for you.

Keep in mind that over time you will discover just how much cross-contamination you can tolerate, so only impart the necessary information. You don't want to overwhelm your host. Remember that you want to have a break occasionally and have someone else cook for you so try to make the task seem simple and easy to accomplish.

1. Offer to buy the gluten-free equivalent of common sauces, spices and mainstays like pasta which are very expensive.

2. Ask them to keep the packaging of whatever processed product they have used in cooking your food.

3. Never assume that their version of your favorite food is the same as yours. Case in point, I don't put Worcestershire sauce in my burgers or my meat pie, but some people do.

4. Ask them to prepare your meal aside from the regular food either by making it first or last after a thorough clean up. There is less chance of cross-contamination if this is done.

5. Remind them that your crackers and bread cannot be mixed into the same basket as regular ones.

6. They need to use a different spoon to check for doneness when testing your food.

7. If they are serving pasta, bring your own strainer.

8. If toast is on the menu bring toaster bags, available at health food stores.

9. I suggest that you always eat a sizable snack before you go to any event. That way if you cannot eat the food, you won't pass out from hunger or have to leave the party to go and get some food.

10. Bring your own jam, peanut butter and/or mayonnaise.

I once brought my own peanut butter to a girl's weekend. A few of us were up early enjoying coffee and toast, using my peanut butter. A late riser rushed into the kitchen, talking the entire time and proceeded to butter her wheat toast with margarine and then before I could stop her, she jammed the crumb-laden knife into my jar.

Everyone at the table gasped. I felt so bad for the poor lady who I had only just met. I gifted the all-natural peanut butter to her, and we laughed about it.

Mistakes will happen and it is best to just laugh it off and save a relationship rather than getting angry.

Chapter 7: Be Kind When Educating

"Respect is one of the greatest expressions of love." -
Don Miguel Ruiz

What's the issue?
Rude and Uninvited

It's hard not to be upset when your health is at hand and someone inadvertently destroys your food. Especially if you're overly hungry. But the quickest way to make sure that this never happens again is to be so rude that you're no longer invited to parties or any occasion where food is present. You can't expect people to remember your sensitivity to gluten, so you must be ready to educate with a smile. When you turn down the offering, you must present your reasoning in a kind-hearted manner, preferably to the host in private. When we cook for others, we are giving of ourselves and a rejection can feel awful, especially if it is done in a rude, insensitive way.

Why does it matter?
Do Your Part to Make the World Gluten-Free Friendly

When we educate people properly, that makes them better citizens of the world at large. Just in the last five years alone, there are so many more choices in restaurants and food products for people with sensitivities and this will only get better if we are kind when educating the regular eaters. If you take your frustrations out on the server in a restaurant, they may jeopardize your ability to eat there safely. Always ask to speak to the manager.

We want people to associate ease and healthy, happy living with the term gluten-free. If we act like know-it-alls and neglect to share valuable insights into our experience in this world, we give ourselves a bad name and conversely make our lives harder.

What you can do today
Six Simple Strategies

1. Always bring a snack for yourself. A granola bar, dried fruit, or small can of soup to avoid hunger and crankiness.
2. Call ahead to a restaurant or visit their website for menu restrictions.
3. Always offer to bring a side dish so you can show people how delicious gluten-free eating can be.
4. Offer to share your recipes with anyone who expresses interest.
5. KISS: Keep it simple silly. They don't need a science lecture. Just share relevant information.

Chapter 8: Stock Your Freezer

"What you do today can improve all of your tomorrows." - Ralph Martson

What's the issue?
Handling Food Cravings

Cravings are a normal part of modern living. We are constantly bombarded in the media by images of junk food and occasionally we need to succumb and have fun. The problem is, most allergy sufferers I know can't just whip up food on a whim at the best of times. It takes quite a bit of time to cook our food from scratch and we often need specialty ingredients to pull off gluten-free versions of popular comfort foods.

Even if you crave a healthy meal but one that is made by someone else, that takes its toll as well. Going out to eat is an effort and allergy sufferers must be in the right frame of mind to take the chance that the experience might leave them sick. And our partners are not always interested or capable of cooking food that is safe for us.

Therefore, I suggest putting some meals in the freezer, even if they are store bought and safe for you to eat.

Why does it matter?
Risky Behavior

Your goal is to get your life back to normal but if we don't plan for food cravings, we can end up sabotaging our efforts.

Before your allergy appeared, you would order pizza occasionally to give yourself a break. Everyone needs to be able to take a night off from cooking. If you don't plan ahead by stocking your pantry or fridge with a few quick meal options, you are more likely to take risks by eating fast food that might not be completely gluten-free.

Without a well-stocked freezer, you are more likely to stop at the restaurant on the way home. Gluten-free food from restaurants is usually far more expensive. If gluten-free eateries are far away from your location when hunger strikes, you are more likely to shop impulsively at a popular hangout that could be unsafe and bring on weeks of aggravating symptoms.

What you can do today
Four Fast Fixes

1. Make extra when you cook so that you can put some away, but this can be tricky with gluten- free baking especially. So as soon as the food has cooled, I put some away in the freezer for a rainy day.

2. Most grocery stores have gluten-free freezer sections where you can find prepared meals and desserts of all kinds. The food is generally very expensive, but it is worth picking up something that you can toss in the oven for a quick meal. Gluten-free pizza has come a long way in recent years, and it is quite yummy. They usually stock fruit pies and ice cream too!

3. Buy prepared soups and stews and broth. We all know that these are invaluable when we are not feeling well and need a warm boost. They are worth their weight in gold.

4. Purchase a bag of your favorite gluten-free cookies and keep them in a sealed container in the back of the cupboard for those days when you need a little boost and a cup of tea

Chapter 9: Food Testing

"Ever tried. Ever failed. No matter. Try again. Fail again. Fail better." Samuel Beckett

What's the issue?
Taking the Hit

After living symptom-free for a period of time you're going to want to try eating some of the foods that once gave you pleasure. Living in a world that is full of fun, fast food that is off limits can lead to feelings of deprivation which can be hard to ignore.

I'm quite guilty of falling off the healthy eating wagon occasionally, particularly when I'm under stress. This means that I will reach for a bag of chips or a piece of chocolate from a brand that I haven't had since going gluten-free. In desperate moments you might find yourself questioning just how much gluten there could be in that hot dog or in those home fries?

My advice is to try one treat at a time and wait to see if you have an adverse reaction before trying a different food. For the most part this is easy to accomplish, unless you find yourself at a party where all sorts of temptations await. In my weak moments, I have given in and tried everything offered to me and then ended up with a rash, unable to pinpoint what the culprit might have been.

I lovingly call it, "taking the hit." I purposely put my skin health at risk by taking a chance that the food in question will bring on a rash. It is a conscious decision done in the name of research and can't be done well if I try too many foods at once.

Why does it matter?
Doing it Right Can Get You Ahead

Remember that your goal is to get your life back to normal and even though that means avoiding all sources of gluten you need to do some testing to discover your tolerance threshold. Being a responsible scientist is the key. It can take a full twenty-four hours for my rash to appear, but you might experience other symptoms more rapidly. When you are manifesting symptoms, you need to wait for them to disappear before trying another food, so that you get an accurate reading and use the knowledge to help you make informed decisions about your diet.

This can be very hard to do, especially at holiday time when you are attending work parties and social events where food is being served. I have ended up in a full-blown rash cycle after attending a few parties in a row. This leaves me feeling discouraged and unsure about which foods I should now avoid. It always seems like a good idea at the time when you are symptom free but testing needs to be methodical so try things one at a time and then slowly your food choices will expand, and your life will become more enjoyable.

What you can do today
Three Helpful Tactics

1. Graciously decline and inform your host that as much as you would like to indulge in their fabulous food, you are in a test phase and have to see how your body responds to one treat at a time, but that you hope to be able to have some at the next opportunity.

2. If you have begun a test and must attend a party, bring an item that is safe for you that you can share with everyone. This way you can mingle and feel a part of the event even if you are not

able to eat the food provided by the host.

3. You may ask for a doggie bag if you know the person very well, explaining that you are so grateful for the chance to taste their cooking but that you must wait until tomorrow to eat it. I have one friend who was honored that I wanted to do this, so it is good to ask. She was happy to send the squares home with me and eager to know how the test went.

Chapter 10: Handling Hecklers

"Only the educated are free." Epictetus

What's the issue?
Resistance to Change

This may be the last chapter in my book but in some ways, I consider it to be the most important.

There is a small percentage of the population who are very confrontational about gluten-free eaters. As I explained in an earlier chapter, food is very personal, and people can feel threatened by anyone who eats differently. Thankfully, I have built my life around like-minded individuals, so I rarely experience this but today I attended a pot-luck brunch, to which I was invited, and I brought some mini gluten-free muffins to share. While perusing the buffet table, I realized that there was nothing that I could eat. One of the organizers pointed to a bowl of fruit salad. I happily filled my bowl and dug in only to learn later that the chef may have put a few splashes of liquor into the bowl with the fruit. This is an excellent example of how you need to ask before you indulge and not assume that fruit salad means only fruit!

I approached the lady who had made the salad in question asking her to give me a better idea of the ingredients. She was very accommodating but another lady sitting at her table was quite rude. She appeared to be exasperated that I would think that anything was wrong with the salad and insisted that even if there was gluten mixed into the fruit, it surely couldn't be enough to hurt anyone! As I had just finished editing chapter 7, which is all about being kind when educating others, I did my best to be diplomatic.

I explained in a non-confrontational manner that any amount of gluten can be a problem. Instead of expressing concern for my situation she appeared to doubt my credibility and turned away. This inspired a third person at the table to jump to my defense which caused a bit of a commotion and the last idea brought forward was, "someone who has allergies takes their chances and their health in their hands when they try to eat at events like these and/or common fast food type establishments." While I agree with this sentiment, it is exactly the kind of thinking that leads someone like me to stay home and not interact with others.

Occasionally, you will run into people who don't understand your allergy. These people might try to minimize your situation and make you feel like you're being overly dramatic and concerned with gluten. You must be your own best advocate. Educate others where you can and walk away from obstinate people. You must take care of yourself so you can be there to take care of the people that you love, and being bed ridden with symptoms distracts us from the activities that we enjoy.

In my case, the reaction I get is mostly hidden on the back of my thighs. I try not to scratch in public, so no one knows that I am having an issue unless I mention it. This works against me because there are no visible signs of my allergy. I don't sneeze (unless I'm in a kitchen where wheat flour is being mixed up) or have trouble breathing or swell up. Because people can't see my symptoms, they wrongly assume that I'm fine.

I once had a cousin say that he thinks people asking for gluten-free food are just looking for attention. This could not be farther from the truth in my case. I long for the good old days when eating was easy, less expensive and carefree.

Why does it matter?
Good Community

It is important to accommodate diversity because we are stronger together than apart. For the record, my allergy only manifested itself when I was forty-five years old and I am indebted to the places and people who offer safe food and safe places for me to visit. Change is hard but when we extend a hand to someone who is different and take the time to make them comfortable, we make the world a better place one person at a time.

What you can do today
Five Ideas to Put an End to Heckling

Occasionally you will find yourself amid hecklers. Here are a few points that might put an end to their attack.

1. I'm allergic and must eat this way. This is neither a choice nor a fad that I am following.
2. The wheat of today is not the same as what was being grown fifty years ago. It has been genetically modified to resist disease. This might be why so many of us cannot tolerate gluten today.
3. Gluten-free food is very expensive so I wouldn't be choosing this lifestyle if I could eat like you.
4. I feel healthier and happier on this diet. Why do you want to take that away from me? Or why does that threaten you?
5. You might feel even healthier than you already do, if you took gluten out of your diet for thirty days.

Beth's Recipes

"Sometimes you just want a brownie!" – Beth Oldfield

Eating should be enjoyable and when you first go gluten-free and try prepared gluten-free, processed food you discover how awful much of it tastes. Everything that I made initially was terrible but I was determined to get my life back on track because I love cooking and baking for my family, and I also wanted to be able to have a sweet treat once in a while that didn't taste like sawdust or cost me a fortune.

The biggest challenge is often breakfast because in North America, we're used to eating bread and cereal products first thing in the morning, so I've included some of my favorite recipes for the weekday rush or the Sunday brunch. I suggest that you make extra and freeze single serving portions that you can grab and go when time is short.

When it comes to lunch and dinner you just need to remember to use only gluten-free sauces and spices in your cooking. I often use lettuce leaves in place of bread in sandwiches. I have used sliced sweet potatoes baked as large coins in place of hamburger buns.

The one bonus of going gluten-free is you have no choice but to turn to vegetables to fill you up. I became much healthier because of this change to my diet. Simply sautéing fresh peppers and onions and zucchini and serving it on rice or quinoa is a great lunch or dinner.

The next hurdle to overcome is baking. I have given you my tried and true recipes to satisfy any sweet tooth. To my delight the biggest compliment I get when someone eats my baking is "this is gluten-free?" Most people are surprised at how good it tastes.

You will notice that many of the recipes are labelled "Mom's." My mother was an amazing cook so much of what I make is based upon the food that I ate as a child. My mother died in 2007. I often wish that she could taste her recipes made gluten-free. It would have been fun to experiment together in the kitchen.

I hope that these recipes help to restore a sense of normalcy to your life. Please read Chapter 3 before attempting these recipes.

Enjoy!

The Breakfast Challenge

It can be quite challenging to come up with good options for breakfast on a gluten-free diet. Most of us are pressed for time in the morning so cooking from scratch is rarely an option. Store bought gluten-free cereal, bread, bagels, English muffins and croissants are very expensive so it's hard to justify the cost, however I do buy some of the above and keep them on hand (often in the freezer) for days when I'm running late. Remember to freeze the homemade leftovers into single servings so you can have a variety of breakfast foods ready to serve.

In this section, I have included some of my favorite recipes for breakfast but here are five quick ideas that need no directions.

1. Greek yogurt is a great tasting alternative to breakfast cereals. I buy unsweetened, lactose-free Greek yogurt and I add maple syrup and berries to make it palatable.
2. All-natural peanut butter on rice cakes or corn cakes.
3. Quinoa porridge made with quinoa flakes by GOGO Quinoa. I top this with fruit and maple syrup.
4. Oatmeal made from certified gluten-free oats, topped with maple syrup and fruit.
5. Protein packed, prepared cereal. I love Pro Granola by Julian Bakery. I eat it with lactose-free cow's milk or almond milk and fruit.

Wake Me Up Smoothie

I bring this smoothie with me for the day and sip it as I teach, that is if it lasts the car ride to work. I find that this wakes me up more than coffee ever did!

I buy a big bag/box of fresh, washed spinach and I put it into plastic bags (you could use containers too) and freeze it so that I can easily grab a handful to put into this smoothie.

The truth is I'm the only one who eats spinach regularly so if I don't freeze it, it rots because I can't eat it fast enough. I also like my smoothies to be very cold, so using frozen ingredients results in a chilled drink. I carry it around in a thermos to keep it cold for as long as possible.

I use a Magic Bullet to blend my smoothie, but any blender will do. You will need to play around with the proportions to get the taste that you like! Substitute any fruit you like. Be creative - you might find a combination that you like better. Just remember to include the hemp hearts as a good source of protein.

Large handful of spinach at least 1 cup – I often pack more in to get a greener drink.
½ cup of prepared orange juice or freshly squeezed
½ cup frozen mango chunks
¼ of a small banana
½ cup of water
2 to 3 tbsp of hemp hearts

Blend the spinach, fruit, juice and water together until smooth and then add the hemp hearts, blending only for 30 seconds.

Beth's Banana Bread

It took me quite a while to come up with a banana bread recipe that worked well. This recipe takes about 15 minutes to throw together and 30 minutes to bake, so it is ideal for a Sunday brunch. I serve it with scrambled eggs and fruit.

Preheat the oven to 350° F.
Grease three 5.75" x 3" pans with butter.

> 2 cups of Bob's Mills Baking Flour
> 2 ½ ripe large bananas mashed to equal 1 cup or a bit more
> ½ cup of granulated sugar (I have also used half brown sugar with good results)
> ½ cup softened butter
> 2 eggs
> 2 tbsp milk (I use Natrel 1% Lactose Free cow's milk)
> ½ tsp vanilla
> 1 ¼ tsp baking powder
> 1 tsp baking soda
> ½ tsp sea salt

Combine the dry ingredients together in a medium mixing bowl.
In a mixer with the paddle attachment, mix the butter and the sugar. Add the eggs, vanilla, bananas and milk. Mix to blend, scraping the bowl down periodically. Add the flour mixture to the wet ingredients and mix on low until combined well.
Fill the greased tins about ¾ of the way from the top and bake for 30-35 minutes or until risen and golden brown. Test with a toothpick in the center. It should come out clean!

Let cool before trying to slice, if you can wait that long!

Date Orange Muffins

Makes 12

These are my favorite muffins because they can be served for brunch or breakfast to someone running out the door in a hurry. I only discovered this recipe after my Mom had died but I know that she would have loved it because of her fondness for dates. Recently, I have started placing a large piece of date on top of the muffin before baking because I like the crunchy, toasted taste of the date.

> 1 orange, unpeeled and cut up in pieces with the seeds removed. (I have also used a large tangerine)
> ½ cup prepared orange juice
> ½ cup chopped dates (seeds removed)
> 1 large egg
> ½ cup softened butter
> 1 ¾ cups Bob's Mills Baking flour
> Scant ¾ cup of granulated sugar (don't pack or fill to the top)
> 1 tsp baking powder
> 1 tsp baking soda

Preheat oven to 400° F.

Grease muffin tin with butter or use paper liners. I prefer to grease because the outside gets nicely browned.

Sift the dry ingredients together or put into a bowl and whisk them until blended.

Put the orange pieces and juice in a blender and puree.

Scrape down the sides and add the dates, egg and butter and blend but note that it will get quite tough for the blender. You just need to break up all the dates with the blender and then remove the batter, scraping down the sides and bottom and empty into the dry ingredients.

Stir just until blended and fill muffin cups 2/3 full. You might not get exactly 12 depending on how big you make your muffins.

Let cool slightly in the tins and then remove to finish cooling on a rack.

English-Style Pancakes

Makes a bunch depending on the size you like

I live in Quebec, Canada which is a bilingual province. The French make crepes which are very thin, rather large pancakes that can be rolled up with various fillings in the middle. The French word for pancake is crepe but this leads to confusion because growing up in an English household, pancakes were light in texture but thick, round and small, stacked high, buttered and served with maple syrup. So, to avoid confusion, these are those. Fluffy, buttery, sweet yumminess!

Use warm temperature ingredients for best results.

  1 ½ cups Bob's Mills Baking flour
  1 tbsp granulated sugar
  1 tbsp baking powder
  ½ tsp sea salt
  1 large egg beaten
  2 tbsp cooking oil (I use sunflower)
  1 ½ cup milk (I use lactose-free cows' milk but almond milk has worked as well)

Mix the dry ingredients.
Beat the egg and add the oil and milk, beating until combined
Add the wet to the dry; beat well. There should be air bubbles present.
Add more milk for thinner pancakes.
Heat a fry pan until water bounces off the surface over medium heat.
Oil the pan sparingly and add ½ cup batter at a time. I can fit 3 in my pan at once. When bubbles appear along the edges, flip or lift to see if it is brown.

Flip and brown other side. Keep warm in an oven until serving.

Classic Coffee Cake

Serves 8-10

Nothing says "I love you" more than warm coffee cake in the morning! This is one of my oldest recipes that is quite a crowd pleaser on a Sunday morning served with scrambled eggs and fresh fruit.

Cake Batter

> 1/3 cup softened butter
> ½ cup granulated sugar
> 1 large egg
> 1 ½ cups Bob's Mills Baking flour
> 2 tsp baking powder
> ½ tsp sea salt
> ¾ cup milk

Topping

> ½ cup brown sugar
> 2 tbsp rice flour
> 1 tsp cinnamon
> 3 tbsp butter melted

Preheat oven to 375° F
Grease an 8" x 8" pan.
Use room temperature ingredients for best results.
Beat the butter and sugar with a mixer until well blended. Add the egg, mixing until combined. Stir the dry ingredients together and then add alternating with the milk, making the last addition dry ingredients.
Mix the topping ingredients and then sprinkle all over the top of the cake.
Bake for 35 minutes or until toothpick comes out clean. Serve warm.

The Best Belgian Waffles

Makes 4 large waffles which we split in two and share.

Waffles are my all-time favorite Sunday breakfast served with strawberries and lactose-free whipped cream. I melt the butter to pour on top for easy spreading and I heat up the maple syrup, so the waffles don't cool down. And always heat your plates.

Heat up your waffle iron, greasing if needed.
Use room temperature ingredients for best results.

> 2 large eggs
> 1 2/3 cup milk (I use lactose-free cows' milk)
> 1/3 cup vegetable oil
> 2 cups Bob's Mills Baking flour
> 1 tbsp baking powder
> 1 ½ tbsp sugar
> ½ tsp sea salt

Whisk the eggs. Add the milk and oil and whisk again.
Stir together the dry ingredients and then add to the milk, mixing very well.
When the waffle iron is hot, fill and cook until the steam almost stops. Remove the waffle with a fork and keep it warm in the oven until they are all ready.

I serve them with melted butter in a pitcher and warmed maple syrup. On special occasions we eat these waffles with lactose-free whipped cream and strawberries.

Sunshine Loaf

Serves 12

This recipe has evolved over the years to become one of my favorite foods to eat with my morning coffee. It's packed with seeds and nuts and is very dense but flavorful. You need to plan ahead because this recipe sits on the counter for 2 hours before you bake it for 30 minutes.

Grease a 9" x 5" loaf pan.

- ½ cup fine grind almond flour
- 1 cup of sunflower seeds
- ½ cup of pecans chopped
- 2 tbsp chia seeds
- ½ cup of whole flaxseeds
- 1 ½ cup quinoa flakes
- 3 tbsp of whole psyllium husks
- 1 ½ tsp of sea salt
- ¾ cup of dried cranberries (I use ones sweetened with apple juice)
- 1 tbsp of honey
- 3 tbsp of melted virgin coconut oil
- 1.5 cups of water

Mix the dry ingredients together in a large bowl. Whisk the wet ingredients together in a measuring cup and then add to the dry. Mix well and let it sit for a bit to get thick.

Pour into a greased loaf pan and press down firmly. I use my grandmother's loaf pan which is a bit wider and longer than a 9" x 5" loaf pan but this will work just as well. You might want to cook it a bit longer for a crunchier bread.

This loaf must sit on the counter for 2 hours.

Preheat the oven to 350° F and bake for 30 minutes.

Remove the loaf from the pan by dumping it out onto a cookie sheet and then slide the loaf back into the oven to cook directly on the rack for another 30 minutes. I like mine to be quite brown, so I have left it for 35 to 40 minutes at times.

You will need to see what you prefer.

Cool completely before slicing.

Sweet Treats

Baking is close to my heart. It's how I show love to my family, especially my kids. When they would arrive home from school, I was that stay-at-home Mom who greeted them with warm cookies and chocolate milk.

I know it sounds cheesy, but I wanted to give my kids what my Mom gave me. When I was little, the school bus would bring us home for lunch so she would have a hot meal ready for me on a TV tray set up on her bed (that was where the television was) and I would get to eat homemade spaghetti or egg salad sandwiches with chips while I watched my favorite cartoons! It was hard to head back to school after such a lovely lunch.

Please read Chapter 3 before trying the following recipes. This will save you lots of misery going forward. I have baked my share of hockey pucks and door stoppers but the recipes I have included in this section will have you smiling from ear to ear right away.

For the most part, I can swap Bob's Mills Baking flour for the wheat flour in my recipes. Once you feel more comfortable baking gluten-free, I suggest you try adapting some of your own recipes using Bob's Mills flours. You just must be ready and willing to throw out the flops if it doesn't quite work out.

Mom's Fudgy Brownies

Serves 12

My Mom used to make the best, super moist, chocolatey brownies. She called them 'Saucepan Brownies' as you only needed one pot to make them. While I can get fairly good results using Bob's Mills Baking flour and her recipe, I have had great reviews with this take on her decadent dessert.

½ cup vegetable oil. I use sunflower
½ cup semi-sweet chocolate chips
½ cup milk chocolate chips
1 cup almond flour
3 tbsp unsweetened cocoa powder (certified gluten-free)
½ tsp baking powder

1 tsp sea salt
3 large eggs
¾ cup granulated sugar
2 tsp of pure vanilla

Preheat oven to 350° F. Grease an 8" x 8" baking pan with butter.
Measure the flour, cocoa, powder and salt into a large bowl. I whisk the ingredients together, but you can sift if you prefer. In another smaller bowl, whisk the eggs, sugar and vanilla together.
In a double boiler, melt the chocolate chips and then add the oil stirring regularly.
When the oil and chocolate are nicely blended, remove from the heat and let cool slightly. Then pour the chocolate mixture into the egg mixture in a steady stream, stirring constantly.
Add the wet ingredients to the dry and stir until thoroughly blended. Pour into a buttered pan.
Bake 30 minutes or until the top is slightly cracked and the brownies have pulled away from the sides. Remove from oven and let them cool completely before cutting. Yes, you can scoop out a piece and eat it, but you will not be able to cut them into nice even squares until they have

cooled. You get the best results when you place them in the fridge before cutting but it's very hard to wait that long. Store in an airtight container.

Mom's Lacy Oatmeal Cookies

Serves 18

I waited quite a while before introducing oats back into my diet because they can still cause a reaction in gluten-sensitive people. I only use certified gluten-free oats.

This is my Mom's recipe for oatmeal cookies and even with regular flour, they are meant to spread until very thin. I call them lacy because my Mom used to crochet doilies which she kept all over the house, and these cookies come out so thin, you can see through them like a doily. You can add more flour to keep them from spreading. I mix these by hand.

½ cup of butter
1 tbsp hot water blended with ½ tsp baking soda
½ cup brown sugar
½ tsp vanilla
½ cup quick cooking gluten-free oats (look for certified gluten-free)
¼ tsp sea salt
½ cup Bob's Mills Baking flour

Preheat oven to 350° F. Line cookie sheets with parchment paper.
Mix the butter and hot water with the baking soda in a large mixing bowl. Add the brown sugar, stirring until combined. Add the vanilla, stir well. Then add the oatmeal, mixing well. Add the flour and salt and mix until completely combined. Drop by the tablespoons onto the parchment keeping in mind that they will spread so I usually only put six on a sheet. Bake for 8 minutes and check on them to make sure that they are not burning.
Add 2-3 minutes of cooking time for them to be dry and golden brown. Remove from the oven and let cool on the trays or lift the parchment paper off the cookie sheets and then leave them to cool on the paper on racks.
Once they have cooled you will be able to lift them up with a cookie

spatula, but it is very hard to wait. Please note that sometimes the cookies spread together so you must cut them up into square cookies. Store in an airtight container.

Chewy Maple Ginger Cookies

Serves 12-14

These cookies are perfect for anyone who loves maple syrup and ginger. For best results use real maple syrup!

¾ cup almond flour
1/3 cup real maple syrup
2 tbsp brown sugar
1 tsp ground ginger

Preheat oven to 350° F
Stir all the ingredients together and chill in the fridge for 10-20 minutes.
Line cookie sheets with parchment paper.
Drop cookies onto the sheet making them as big as you desire. I keep mine on the smaller side so that I can get more of them.
Press them down with the palm of your hand to keep them flat, or if you prefer a slightly underdone cookie than leave them in mounds.
Bake for 10-12 minutes or until they appear dry around the edges.
No matter how long you keep them in the oven, they will always come out chewy.
Let them cool on the trays if you can wait!
Store in an airtight container.

Best-Ever Chocolate Chip Cookies – *No Really*

Serves 18-24

My kids love the gluten-free version of my chocolate chip cookies. I now make them with almond flour because this yields the best results. They are chewy and hard to resist right out of the oven. I have even heard them say that these cookies are better than the ones I used to make before going gluten-free!

> 2 ½ cups of almond flour
> ¾ tsp sea salt
> ½ tsp baking soda
> ½ cup grapeseed oil
> ½ cup maple syrup
> 1 tbsp pure vanilla
> Heaping ½ cup semisweet chocolate chips

Mix the dry ingredients together.
Mix the wet ingredients together.
Then add the wet to the dry and blend well and place in the fridge for 20 minutes.
Preheat oven to 350° F.
Roll into balls and place on tray leaving about 2" between each cookie.
Flatten with a fork or the palm of your hand. Or leave in mounds to get a moister cookie.
Bake 7-10 minutes or until golden brown.
I like my cookies well done but you will need to experiment with this for yourself.

Let cool on sheet completely if you can!

Josh's Birthday Bundt Cake

Serves 12-14

This was my son's favorite birthday cake because he knew that it was made with chocolate syrup -the kind that we used to add to our milk as kids. Because I am leery of what might be in the regular store-bought version, I make my own chocolate syrup using a gluten-free hot chocolate mix that has sugar in it. I start with just a bit of chocolate powder and add water to make a thick syrup until I have ½ cup.

> ¾ cup softened butter
>
> 1 ½ cups of granulated sugar
>
> 3 large eggs
>
> 1 ½ tsp pure vanilla
>
> ¾ cup milk (I use lactose free cows' milk)
>
> 2 ½ cups Bob's Mills Baking flour
>
> 2 tsp baking powder
>
> ½ cup chocolate syrup (I make my own as described above)
>
> ¼ tsp baking soda

Preheat oven to 325° F. Grease a large Bundt pan. All ingredients should be at room temperature for best results. With an electric mixer, beat together the butter, sugar, eggs and vanilla. You want the mixture to be smooth. Slowly add the milk while the mixer is mixing and then continue mixing for about 1 minute.

Stir together the flour and baking powder. Add this to the batter in 4 portions, beating well after each addition.

Pour about 2/3 of the batter into the Bundt pan so that it fills the bottom. Add the chocolate syrup and the baking soda to the remaining batter and beat until combined. Spoon this batter over the top and then using a knife, gently swirl together by lifting the white batter up to the surface with a turn of the wrist.

Bake for 50-70 minutes, checking for doneness when a toothpick inserted into the cake comes out clean.

Allow to cool completely. Gently pull the cake away from the sides with a knife before tipping upside down to remove from the pan. Dust with icing sugar.

Perfect Apple Pie

Serves 8-10

To me the crust on any pie is the most important part. In our house, it is never allowed to be wasted and people must check with me before throwing it out! I always have room for pie crust. I use this crust for any pie, be it pumpkin, strawberry or apple or lemon. I even use this crust for my chicken pot pie!

Pie filling

> 6 cups thinly sliced, peeled apples (I use Cortland)
> ¾ cup granulated sugar
> 2 tbsp rice flour
> ¾ tsp cinnamon
> ¼ tsp sea salt
> Scant ¼ tsp nutmeg (Don't overfill or pack)
> 1 tsp freshly squeezed lemon juice

Stir all the ingredients together and let sit while you mix the pastry.

Pastry

> ½ cup tapioca flour
> ½ cup cornstarch
> ¼ cup arrowroot starch
> 1 cup sweet rice flour
> 1 tsp xanthan gum
> ½ tsp sea salt
> Dash of granulated sugar
> ½ cup of cold butter
> ½ cup vegetable shortening
> 1 large cold egg

1 tbsp vinegar

4 Tbsp ice water

Sift the dry ingredients together and cut in the butter and shortening with a pastry blender until it resembles crumbs.

Stir the wet ingredients together in a measuring cup and then add all at once to the dry. Mix with a fork until it forms a large ball.

Divide in half, pressing between waxed paper to form two individual discs. Refrigerate for an hour. This is very important as the dough is very hard to handle otherwise.

Preheat the oven to 425° F.

Technique:

I have found that the best way to roll pastry is between two pieces of waxed paper.

Remove the dough discs from the fridge and lay a new piece of waxed paper on the table and then put the disc in the center.

Top with another large piece of waxed paper and roll with the rolling pin to get the desired size. You can buy pastry mats that have circles printed on them to get the correct size for your dish.

You must work fast because when the pastry warms up it is hard to handle without breaking.

Transfer to the pie plate by flipping it off the waxed paper onto the plate. It likely will not release all the way on its own, but you should be able to easily peel it off. Then repair any tears in the crust by pressing the dough together.

If you are unable to roll the dough because it has warmed too much, put back in the fridge or simply press the dough into the pie plate evenly.

Add the apple mixture to the pie plate and repeat the process with the top layer of pie crust.

I slit holes in the top crust with a knife. And you can brush with an egg wash to get a nice shine.

Bake for 40-45 minutes until apples are tender and crust is golden brown.

Let cool completely before cutting because otherwise the filling will not set and will run out of the pie when sliced.

Delicious Dinners and Lunches

Dinners and lunches are a bit easier to pull off on a gluten-free diet if you make certain that all the sauces and spices and additives are free from gluten. Because I was worried about the contents of prepared salad dressings, I started making my own and I have included two of them in this section.

Because I found gluten-free bread to be quite expensive, I started eating leftover dinner for lunches almost daily instead of sandwiches. Make big portions of your nightly meal and pack your lunch the night before with your name on it to ensure it is still there in the morning!

Lettuce leaves are a great replacement for sliced bread for sandwiches. You can buy rice tortillas to make wraps and rice cakes are a great bread replacement. Corn cakes are a bit thinner and they don't crumble as easily. I have baked large slices of sweet potato and used them as hamburger buns.

The biggest challenge I faced was finding a good pasta, and the gluten-free equivalent for soy-sauce and Worcestershire sauce. Both tastes quite different from the original so you will miss that flavor, but you can make up for it with spices. I use The Wizard's organic gluten-free vegan Worcestershire sauce and San-J Organic gluten-free soy sauce.

When it comes to pasta, my favorite brand is Tinkyada pasta. This pasta holds up well in sauces and keeps well for next day leftovers.

I have included some easy recipes for dinners which make great leftovers for lunch.

Enjoy!

Beth's Balsamic Maple Salad Dressing

I whip this together quickly whenever I want to season my salad. I only make enough for a single use. Feel free to adapt at will. It is very forgiving. I pour all the ingredients into a container with a lid and then shake it until it combines well.

3 tbsp olive oil
1 to 2 tbsp balsamic vinegar
1 to 2 glugs of maple syrup to taste
½ tsp of minced garlic
Sea salt and pepper to taste

Pour into a container with a tight-fitting lid and shake until combined. Store in the fridge for two to three days.

Simple Caesar Salad Dressing

I don't know where I found this recipe, but it is wonderful. I love parmesan cheese, so I often put extra into this recipe. I mix the ingredients together in a mason jar that has a lid and I store it in the fridge for a week. You can toast up some gluten-free bread garlic bread, break it into cubes and toss on top of the salad. Just double the portions if you want to make more.

1 ½ cloves of minced garlic (I use the kind that is sold in the jar already minced in oil)

1 tbsp freshly squeezed lemon juice

½ tsp Dijon mustard

½ tsp gluten-free Worcestershire sauce

½ cup of mayonnaise

¼ cup of grated parmesan cheese (I use fresh, lactose-free cheese, not the stuff sold in a can)

¼ tsp of sea salt

Pinch of black pepper

Put everything into a mason jar. Stir with a spoon until combined and then store in the fridge for one week.

Marvelous Mango Stew

Serves 8-10

This was the very first gluten-free dinner that I made for my family. It was a big hit and now I must double the recipe to ensure there are leftovers for lunches. You can be creative with the ingredients and portions. This recipe is very forgiving.

    1 14 oz can diced tomatoes
    1 large sized sweet potato
    1 large red onion diced
    1 large red pepper chopped
    2 cloves of garlic minced
    1 tsp chili flakes
    1 can -16 oz of kidney beans undrained
    1 can- 16 oz of black beans undrained
    1 ½ cups of frozen mango chunks
    2 tbsp maple syrup to cut the sharp taste of the tomatoes – optional
    Fistful of chopped parsley – optional
    1 tsp of sea salt
    ½ tsp of black pepper

In a large pot, heat two tablespoons of oil – I use avocado oil, but any will do.
Sauté the onions until translucent. Add the garlic and sauté for 2-3 minutes stirring often so the garlic doesn't burn.
Add the canned tomatoes, peppers, potatoes, chili flakes, salt and pepper. Simmer for 25 minutes.
Add the beans, mango and parsley.
Cook for 15 minutes and then serve on rice.

Mom's Mac and Cheese – Lactose Free

Serves 4

My Mom loved this dinner and she would serve it with pickled beets. When I was very little, she used to put crushed tomatoes into the mixture. I prefer it like this. The older the cheese the better as old cheese has a great, strong flavor.

1 cup of elbow macaroni – I use Tinkyada Brown Rice Pasta

1 tsp of butter

1 large egg beaten

½ tsp sea salt

½ tsp black pepper

1 tsp dry mustard

1 tbsp hot water

1 cup lactose-free milk – I use Natrel 1% lactose-free cow's milk

3 cups of lactose-free old cheddar cheese shredded – Black Diamond

Grease a 9" x 9" with butter.

Mix the mustard and salt and water. Heat the milk slightly in a pot on the stove, remove and then add the mustard mixture to it, stirring to blend well.

Boil the macaroni until tender, being sure not to overcook. Drain and stir in the butter and egg.

Add most of the cheese to the macaroni and stir well over the turned-off burner, just to ensure that the cheese melts a bit.

Pour the macaroni into the greased pan, spreading around to create an even layer and then pour the milk mixture over the top. Top with the remaining cheese.

Bake for 30-40 minutes or until the custard is set and top is crusty a bit. You can put the broiler on for the last minute to make it golden and bubbly.

Ellen's Tuna Casserole

Serves 6-8

I loved my Mom-in-law's tuna casserole so much that she used to bake it and wrap it up for me as a Christmas present. I do not like fish, but this dish makes me smile and crave chips! Ellen would serve it with boiled potatoes and peas.

2 cans of undrained tuna
1 can of cream of mushroom soup – I use Aylmer as it is gluten-free
¼ cup of milk – I use Natrel 1% lactose free cow's milk
¼ cup finely chopped yellow onion
½ tsp sea salt
Big dash of black pepper
250 grams of fettuccini – I use La Veneziane fettuccee corn pasta

Preheat oven to 350° F.
Grease a 9" x 9" covered casserole dish.
You might have to play with this recipe a bit depending on the type of pasta that you use. The package of corn pasta that I buy comes in mounds and I use 5 of them in this recipe.
You could mix part of the pasta with the rest of the ingredients and if it seems too runny adjust by adding more pasta, and if you want it to be creamier, add more milk.
Cook the noodles. Drain.
Mix all the other ingredients together and add the pasta.
Pour into the greased dish and bake for 30 to 40 minutes with the cover on. My mother-in-law likes to cover the top with crushed potato chips before putting it in the oven.

Slow Cooked Beef

Serves 8-10

This meal is prepared in a slow cooker. It cooks for 7 hours at least. The last hour is when the magic happens. I have tried cooking it for 6 hours but it's not as tender. You can serve it with your favorite vegetables or rice.

2-3-pound blade roast
1 large yellow onion chopped
2 cups of beef bouillon
Sea salt
Black pepper
2 tsp minced garlic

Sauté onion until it is caramelizing. Remove from the pan and place in the bottom of the slow cooker.
Pat the beef with paper towel so that is dry before browning on all sides in butter. Put it on top of the onions in the slow cooker.
Use enough beef bouillon to fill the slow cooker only halfway up the sides of the beef.
Set to cook on low for 7 hours. Try not to peek or lift the lid to keep the heat in during cooking.
Serve over rice or with mashed potatoes and canned petits pois – my Mom's favorite peas.

Credits and Acknowledgements

I would like to thank Margaret Goldik for editing all my manuscripts in a timely, professional manner. Your kindness knows no bounds and I am forever grateful for your support and encouragement.

I would also like to acknowledge the work done by my Virtual Assistant, Joly Masa. Thank you for your help on this project! Contact Joly on Facebook via: The Savvy Fempreneur.

About the Author

Beth resides in a small town located on Mount Rigaud in Quebec, Canada, where she has been living for 25 years with her husband Peter. Together they have designed and built two homes with their own hands and raised three beautiful children. When she is not teaching; reading or writing short stories and updating her weekly fitness blog on her website: betholdfield.ca, she is cooking delicious gluten-free food for her family and friends.

Beth has been teaching fitness for 20 years in Pointe-Claire, Quebec. Beth's mission is to educate and motivate her students to be the best that they can be in body, mind and spirit. Her specialties include Aerobics/Yoga/Step/Muscle Conditioning/Line Dance and Essentrics.

Beth is a Best-Selling Author of:

Fundamental Fitness After Fifty – Three at Home Fitness Programs to Keep You Functionally Fit For Life.

Co-Author of *Shine! Inspirational Stories of Choosing Success Over Adversity. Volume 3.*

Beth's Designations include:

Bachelor of Arts-McGill University

Diploma in Education-McGill University

Best-Selling Author

Fitness Instructor Specialist-canfitpro PRO TRAINER

Personal Trainer Specialist-canfitpro

Older Adult Specialist-canfitpro

Manufactured by Amazon.ca
Bolton, ON